A NEW TYPE OF SHOVEL REMOVING THE TOP SOIL FROM A BLUFF IN THE COTSWOLD HILLS schemes were undertaken. To meet the increasing demands made by these, our old friends the spade and shovel evolved into the most wonderful excavating machines.

At this stage in the evolution of machinery it seems well that there should be some record of the advance we have made up to the present moment in the methods of digging and excavating. With this end in view, and with little other excuse than that no one else seems minded to attempt the task, I have ventured to produce this small collection of drawings for all of those who are interested in the mechanical triumphs of Homo Sapiens. Also it may well prove that future generations will be grateful for such a record, and congratulate themselves on their descent from those gifted forefathers who created the wonderful machines here depicted.

LURED BY A RARE SPECIMEN

Fortune has favoured me in this. Wandering recently in the neighbourhood of the city of Lincoln in search of data for a new work I am compiling on the ravages of the lesser lepidoptera—one of my many side-lines—I was lured by a rare specimen into the mysterious precincts of the Ruston-Bucyrus works. Far from arousing resentment by my intrusion, I was received with open arms by members of the staff, who insisted on my making a tour of inspection of the works. Nothing loth to comply with their courtesy, I meandered as in a wondering dream through the vast playground of their monster and almost incredible creations. So bemused was I with the strangeness of it all that I stumbled into a crater recently made in playful mood by a grabbing crane. Assisted to my feet with the greatest kindness by my conductors, and not without some good-natured merriment at my expense, we resumed our journey.

I STUMBLED INTO A CRATER

It is quite wrong, by the way, to conclude, as some writer whose name escapes me has permitted himself to do in a fit of unbridled

THE GENTLE ART OF ADVERTISING

W. Heath Robinson

Duckworth

First published 1979

Sources of drawings include the following: *The Gentle Art of Excavating* by W. Heath Robinson, issued by Ruston-Bucyrus Ltd, Lincoln (n.d.); *Some Trade Secrets Revealed* by Rogers Peet Company, New York (n.d.); *Behind the Scenes at Moss Bros with Heath Robinson*, issued by Moss Bros. & Co Ltd, Covent Garden, London WC2 (n.d.); *Then and Now*, illustrated by W. Heath Robinson, issued by the Port of Manchester Warehouses Ltd, Trafford Park, Manchester (1921); Prospectus of William Cooke & Co Ltd, Sheffield (n.d.); *The Gentle Art of Reproducing* by W. Heath Robinson issued by the Practical Etching Service Ltd, London EC1 (n.d.); *The Making of Asbestos-Cement Roofing as seen by W. Heath Robinson*, issued by Building Products Ltd, Asbestos House, London SE1 (n.d.)

Gerald Duckworth & Co Ltd
The Old Piano Factory
43 Gloucester Crescent, London NW1

ISBN 0 7156 1428 2

Printed in Great Britain by
Unwin Brothers Limited
The Gresham Press, Old Woking, Surrey, England
A member of the Staples Printing Group

CONTENTS

THE GENTLE ART OF EXCAVATING

JOHNNIE WALKER

SOME TRADE SECRETS REVEALED BY ROGERS PEET COMPANY

BEHIND THE SCENES AT MOSS BROS

THEN AND NOW

COOKE'S WIRE ROPES

THE GENTLE ART OF REPRODUCING

ADVERTISEMENTS

THE MAKING OF ASBESTOS-CEMENT ROOFINGS

MISCELLANEOUS

PREFACE

'Are you legal, decent, honest and truthful? Advertisers have to be', proclaims the Advertising Standards Authority somewhat self-righteously from the hoardings today. Heath Robinson could have claimed to be the first three in everything he did; as to the fourth, he would probably have turned the question lightly aside with one of those characteristic mock-solemn evasions in which his letters abound.

Drawings of industrial processes for advertising purposes were a large and constant part of his work for the last forty years of his life. The heyday was during the 1920s, after the publication of his second children's book *Bill the Minder* (Constable, 1912—we should call it *Bill the Babysitter* if it appeared for the first time today) and the success of his cartoons of the First World War.

Of course it was never quite plain sailing. An enormous variety of different trades and manufactures employed him—coal mines, tanneries, dockyards, cement works, cutlers, tailors, makers of beef tea, Swiss rolls, whisky and boot polish—and his determination to achieve verisimilitude let him in for a personal visit to each. At first he was nervous about caricaturing work processes which seemed to absorb so many serious-looking men so completely; but he was wrong about this. 'When their stern preoccupation with the work was lifted', he wrote, 'these earnest men were like children out of school. Nothing pleased them more than to see that which held them so tyrannically treated with levity.'

Getting his roughs approved was another difficulty. A magazine has only one editor or art editor the artist has to please; a large industrial concern proceeds more cumbrously by a committee of directors, each one of which has to make his own views felt, and this after the artist has done his stuff, never before. One firm suggested in the middle of the proceedings that the office cat should be introduced in the picture of the accounts department, as it always attended the monthly despatch of statements; when Heath Robinson had put it in, the drawing had to be revised yet again, since he had not shown it actually licking the envelopes, as it sometimes liked to do. Constant frustrations attended getting the work done in time—Christmas cards printed in time for Christmas, not after, and so on; and no doubt Heath Robinson's advertising clients took every possible advantage of his unflagging diligence and willingness to oblige.

It is a selection of his multifarious work for these exacting clients that is resurrected in this book. A number of the drawings are graced with Heath Robinson's own added text, in a style of deadpan humour which matches the pictures exactly and is highly characteristic of the man himself. Even the Advertising Standards Authority might be prepared to admit that there is a certain wild truth in these spirited and ingenious productions.

M.H.

The Gentle Art of Excavating

W. HEATH ROBINSON

THE INVENTOR OF THE MECHANICAL SHOVEL TRYING OUT AN EARLY TYPE

The Gentle Art of Excavating

"WHEN Adam delved and Eve span, who was then the gentleman ?" is a question more easily asked than answered, as the mediæval proposer of the riddle appears to have discovered for himself. He provided us with no solution. We may be quite certain that Eve managed her spinning all right, but Adam's delving must have been on the weak side, and anything but a gentle art.

Our remote ancestors, so we are told, used to dig with a piece of stick pointed at the end, or with the shoulder-blade of an ox fastened to the branch of a tree with thongs or beef tendons. These were then, as they are now, tough and capable of much resistance. Victory must have taken a long time in arriving when dug for with implements such as these, and when attained, no doubt, was very gratifying to the Homo Sapiens of the period. He asked for so little from this life.

A PREHISTORIC EXCAVATOR

Some thousands of years after this there was born that unknown genius who invented the shovel and spade. I mean the real spade—the spade that can rightly be called a spade. Whether this bright fellow was a Neanderthal man or a member of the Aurignatian or Magdalenian races, I do not know. In any case, from now on things went as smoothly as could be expected. No important change seems to have occurred in the method of delving or excavating until the arrival of the Machine Age.

Before this, for countless years man had been happy enough with his spade. He dug his barrows on the heath in which he reverently deposited his granddad's bones with a saucer of grape-nuts or other grain food, together with a pitcher of water, to sustain the old man on his journey into the unknown. He dug his narrow trenches to irrigate his allotment, and tilled his little patch of spinach with a contented mind. But now vast and ever vaster engineering

W HEATH ROBINSON
AN IMPROVED
DRAGLINE
CLEARING OUT THE
BOTTOM OF THE
UPPER REACHES OF
THE RIVER THAMES

A NEW MULTI-MOVEMENT
DRAG SHOVEL
EXCAVATING FOR
THE FOUNDATIONS
OF A NEW
CINEMA
SITE
OF THE NEW
SUPER DE LUXE
CINEMA
W. HEATH ROBINSON

THE BEGINNING OF A GARDEN SUBURB
EXCAVATING A NEW ROAD WITH A SPECIALLY DESIGNED SKIMMER
DORISDENE AVENUE
W HEATH ROBINSON

imagination, that because machines grow more powerful and vaster year by year they will eventually overpower their makers. Take, for example, the Electric Shovel. Though with the strength of a giant, what could exceed in obedience its almost childlike response to the driver in the luxuriously appointed cab? It scoops up great masses of earth at the bidding of its master as easily as you or I spoon up our porridge at breakfast. As I watched it at work it all seemed so simple. I felt that I could work the machine myself, and was a little chagrined that I was not invited to do so. The Drag Shovel is also a model of obedience with an old-world air of courtesy as it bows its long boom to the earth with which it is about to deal.

THE MULTIPLEX DRAGLINE FOR DRAGGING WINDING STREAMS — ANOTHER SUGGESTION BY MR. W HEATH ROBINSON

The Skimmer is a machine used in the making of roads. Its skimming is a joy to behold. So true is the action of this delightful machine that, so I was told, it can skim off the jam from a slice of bread and jam without disturbing the butter. My conductors regretted that they could not perform this test for my edification, as a slice of bread and jam could not be found in the whole of the works.

TREASURE TROVE

The Dragline must be seen to be believed, with its graceful "come hither" action, while the Grabbing Crane deserves a chapter to itself. I have only one fault to find with the Grabbing Crane, and that is its name. It somehow brings to mind those marauders who gain a precarious living by snatching and grabbing from shop windows. I never quite believed the story that one of these machines was used by an unscrupulous gang of this description. Far from deserving so evil a reputation, the Grabbing Crane may be described as a Machine with a Conscience. It is quite true that it has a habit of lifting things which rightly do not belong to it, but on the other hand it faithfully deposits those things where the rightful owner

THE LATEST
TYPE OF
GRAB CRANE
CLEARING OUT A
SMALL POND ON
HAMPSTEAD HEATH
W HEATH ROBINSON

MOHAMMED AND THE MOUNTAIN

wishes them to be placed. Nothing is too large for its grasp. Had Mohammed possessed a Grabbing Crane he would have had no difficulty in bringing the mountain to him and thus have saved an unnecessary and tiresome walk.

Perhaps I was most deeply moved by the Walking Dragline, or Bucyrus-Monighan, as it is sometimes called. There is something so playful and even skittish in its peregrinations. Yes, I must confess to a weakness for this fascinating machine, and I have long wished to own one. This weakness was shared by an old friend of mine who once bought a Bucyrus-Monighan in which, with his family, he spent a summer holiday. He tells me that he found the long boom so useful in bathing and diving when the machine came to rest on the beach. The only drawback was the confinement of the sleeping quarters, due to the presence of the machinery. However, the children found the latter very amusing on rainy days.

THE CORNER GRAB CRANE FOR WORKING ROUND CORNERS
A VALUABLE SUGGESTION BY Mr W. HEATH ROBINSON NOW UNDER CONSIDERATION BY RUSTON-BUCYRUS LTD.

It should be stated here that the Ruston-Bucyrus Ltd., while raising no objection whatever to the use of the machine in this way, wish it to be clearly understood that it is not made for this sort of thing. Its rightful use is far different from this. Like the other machines made by the Ruston-Bucyrus Ltd., it can move mountains, and by a process of addition, make mountains out of molehills.

I regret that the scarcity of paper will not permit me to include in this brochure the many other achievements of Ruston-Bucyrus Ltd., but enough has been shown, I hope, to record how far we have travelled on the road of progress since the far-off days when Adam delved and Eve span.

W. HEATH ROBINSON

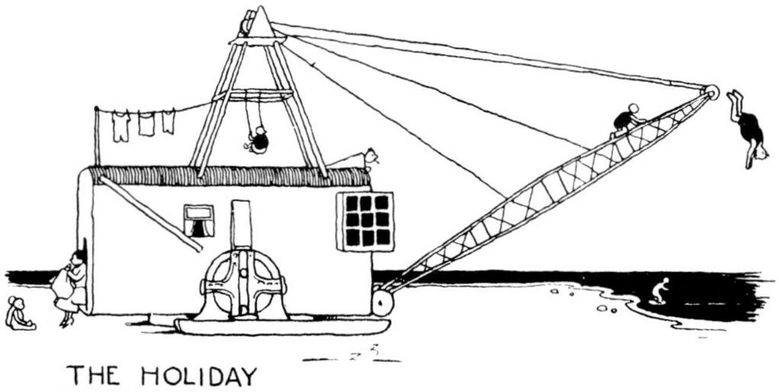

THE HOLIDAY MONIGHAN DRAGLINE

W HEATH ROBINSON
PRIVATE
AN EARLY FORM OF THE
WALKING DRAGLINE STRIPPING ROCKY
OVERBURDEN PREPARATORY TO ERECTING
A NEW TEA SHOP IN THE
ALLEGHANY MOUNTAINS

Squaring the 'Johnnie Walker' Bottles

Designing the well-known get-up of 'Johnnie Walker' in the 'Johnnie Walker' Studios

 The 'Johnnie Walker' Cask Expert Testing the Soundness of a Cask

In the 'Johnnie Walker' Filling Cellars

In the Filtering Vaults at Kilmarnock

The 'Johnnie Walker' experts testing whisky samples with the patent testing dial in the sample room

Subjecting Cloth to Rogers Peet's Ingenious Sheepdog Test for All Wool

Clans of MacRogers and MacPeet Rounding-up Mist for Rogers Peet's
Scotch Mist Cloth

A Busy Afternoon in the Weighing Yards of Rogers Peet's Solight Hat Department

Obtaining Style Reactions at the Monthly Meeting of the Rogers Peet Company's Board of Directors

Up-to-Date Tie Tests employed by Messrs. Rogers Peet Company

Research Work by Rogers Peet's Expert Detectives to obtain Data on which to base their Famous 85 Percenter Last for Shoes

As you can see, we go to absurd lengths to ensure that no one can say of our cloth that its warp is worse than its woof

When Rabelais wrote 'Revenons à nos boutons' he had undoubtedly suffered one of those social misadventures from which our customers are happily exempt

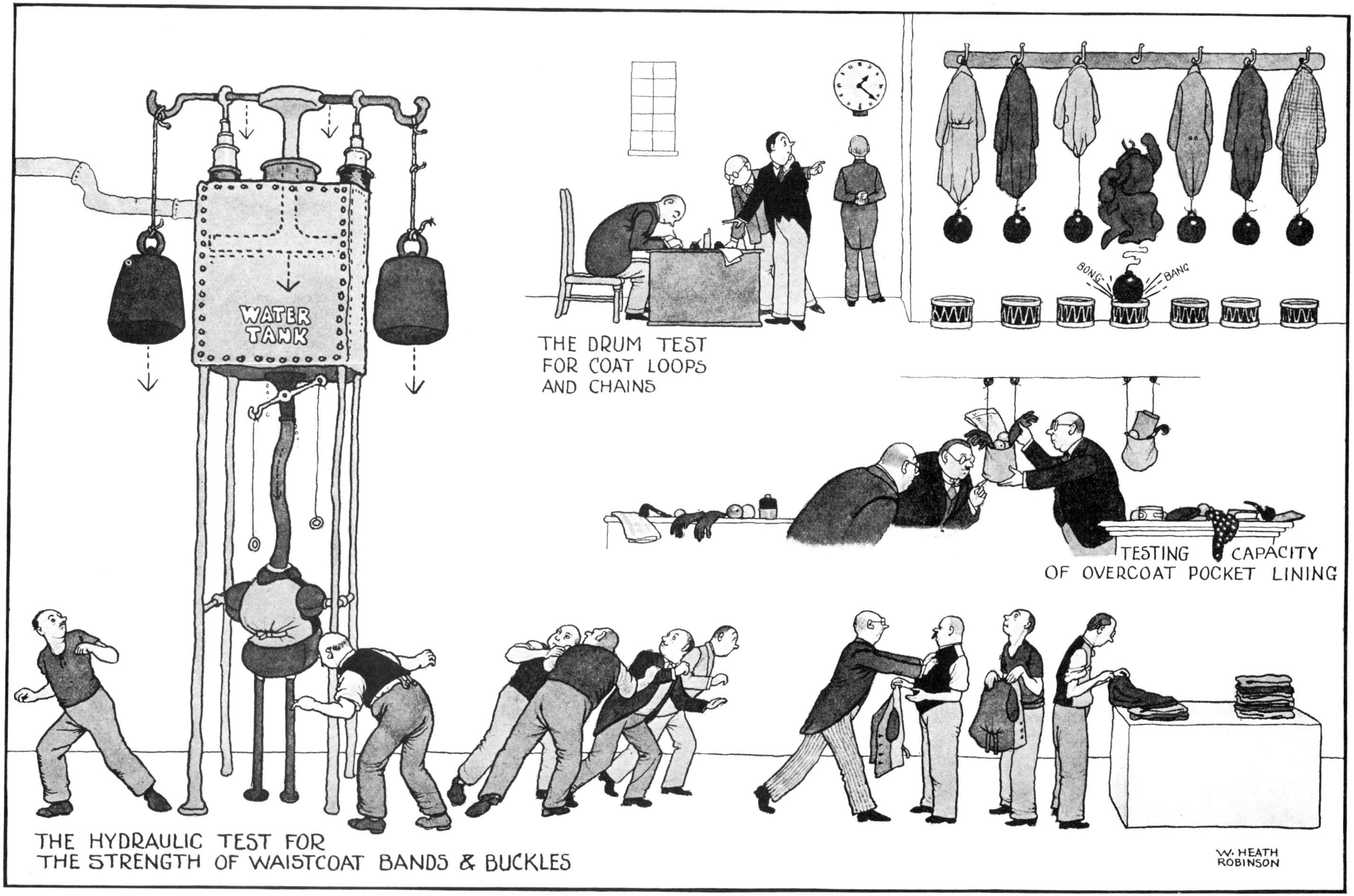

The man responsible for the strength of our coat loops has recently been consulted by the builders of a famous suspension bridge

The staff of our Olfactorium are all men of international repute. They are insured at Lloyd's for many thousands of pounds against the common cold

Even when it rains cats and dogs you'll find our waterproofs a complete protection against claw and paw (and, of course, down-paw)

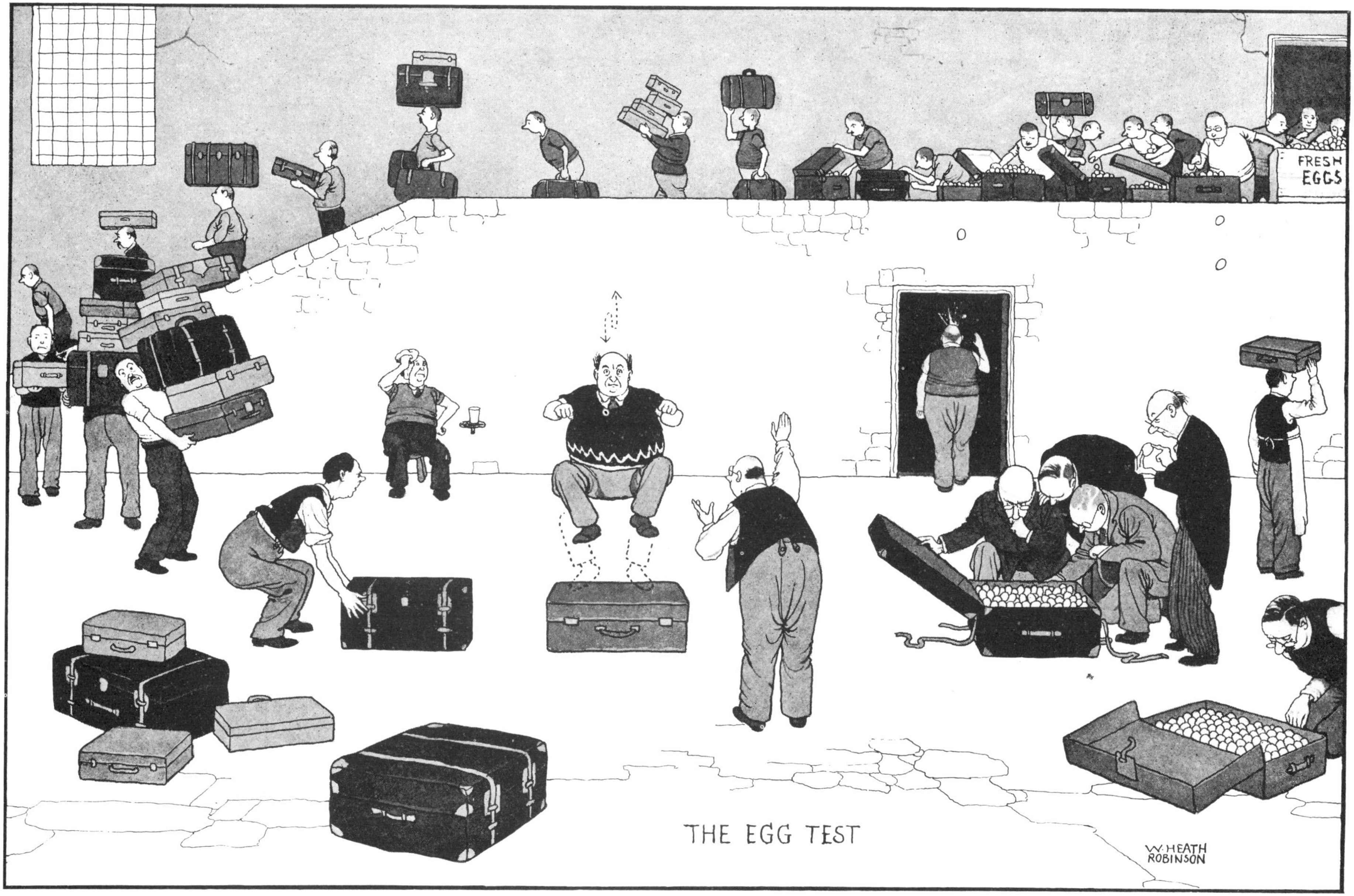

Our hens used to dread a trunk-call, but now they have learned to have complete confidence in our wares

IN THE TRYING ON DEPT.
EXAMINING THE BACK
FITTING OF A PAIR OF
RIDING BREECHES

After this peep into the back of beyond you can confidently lead the field knowing that all will be well behind you

You will find it impossible to upset our Breeches Buoys (bless them!) however much you try it on

Those week-end cottages are all very well, but most of us like a little more luxury in our country seat

Arms and the man present no terrors to our students once they have taken their third degree at our Academy of Salesmanship

MOSS BROS de Luxe . . . Our Emporium is exactly like this except for the palms, fountains, pillars,

stage, staircase, etc., etc. . . . But really—it's a very comfortable place in which to choose a suit

Last December our Christmas delivery was mistaken for a fog. Our aim is so sure that we can drop your new top-hat accurately on to your head

This is not *quite* the shape of things to come at MOSS BROS . . . but we really have the builders in—actually working!

Supposed origin of the warehouse—an early effort to preserve a filbert through the winter months

Congestion arising from manhandling

Sectional view of old fashioned manhandled warehouse with stories

One of the old machines for counting and checking peas after haulage

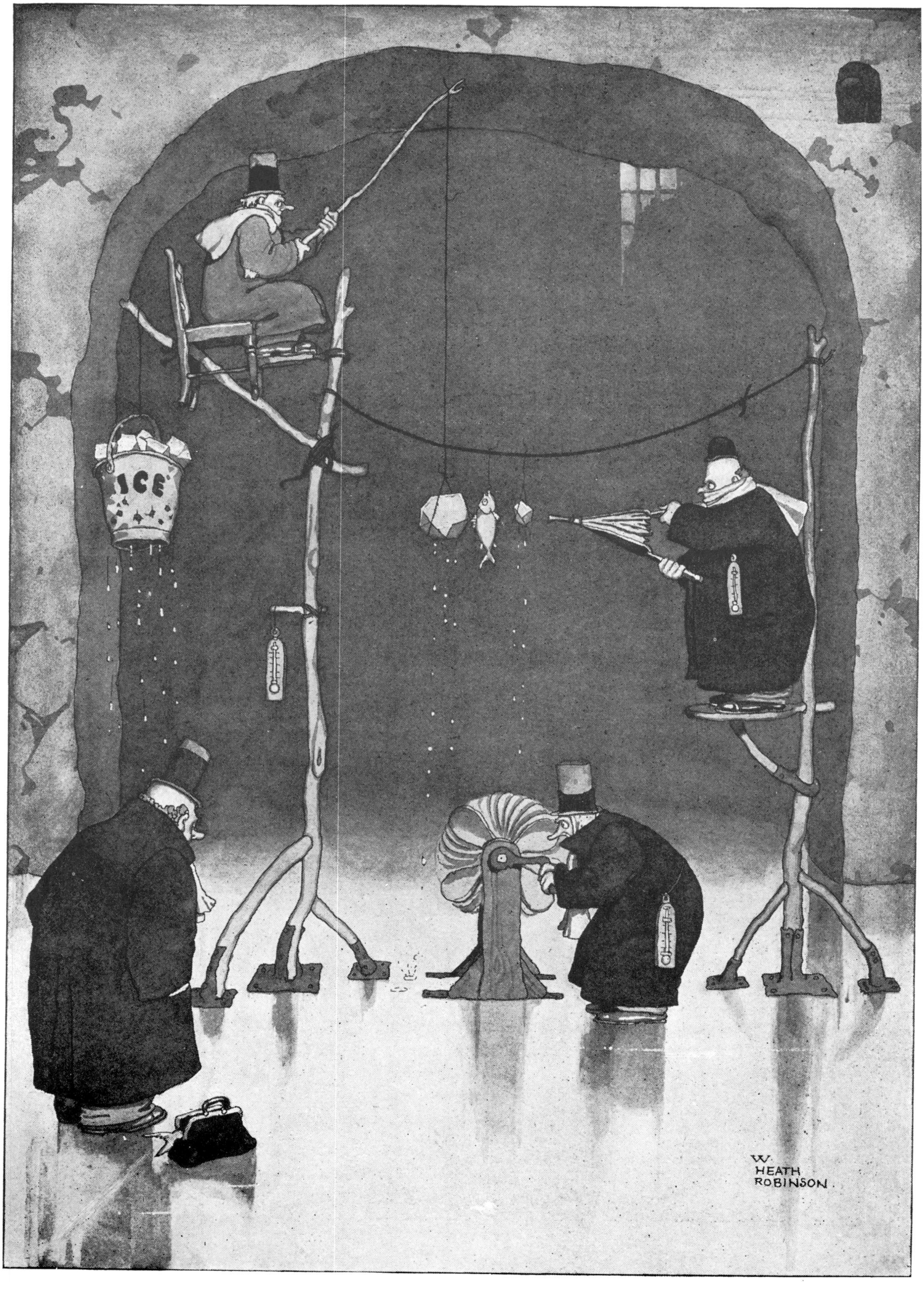

An old and somewhat laborious method of refrigerating a fresh herring

A dream of the future

Some tests for drawn wire

A very early stranding machine

A tense moment when testing the strength of the finished rope

Easier splicing with the new super-magnetic labour-saving splicer

The latest machinery for the mass production of horseshoes

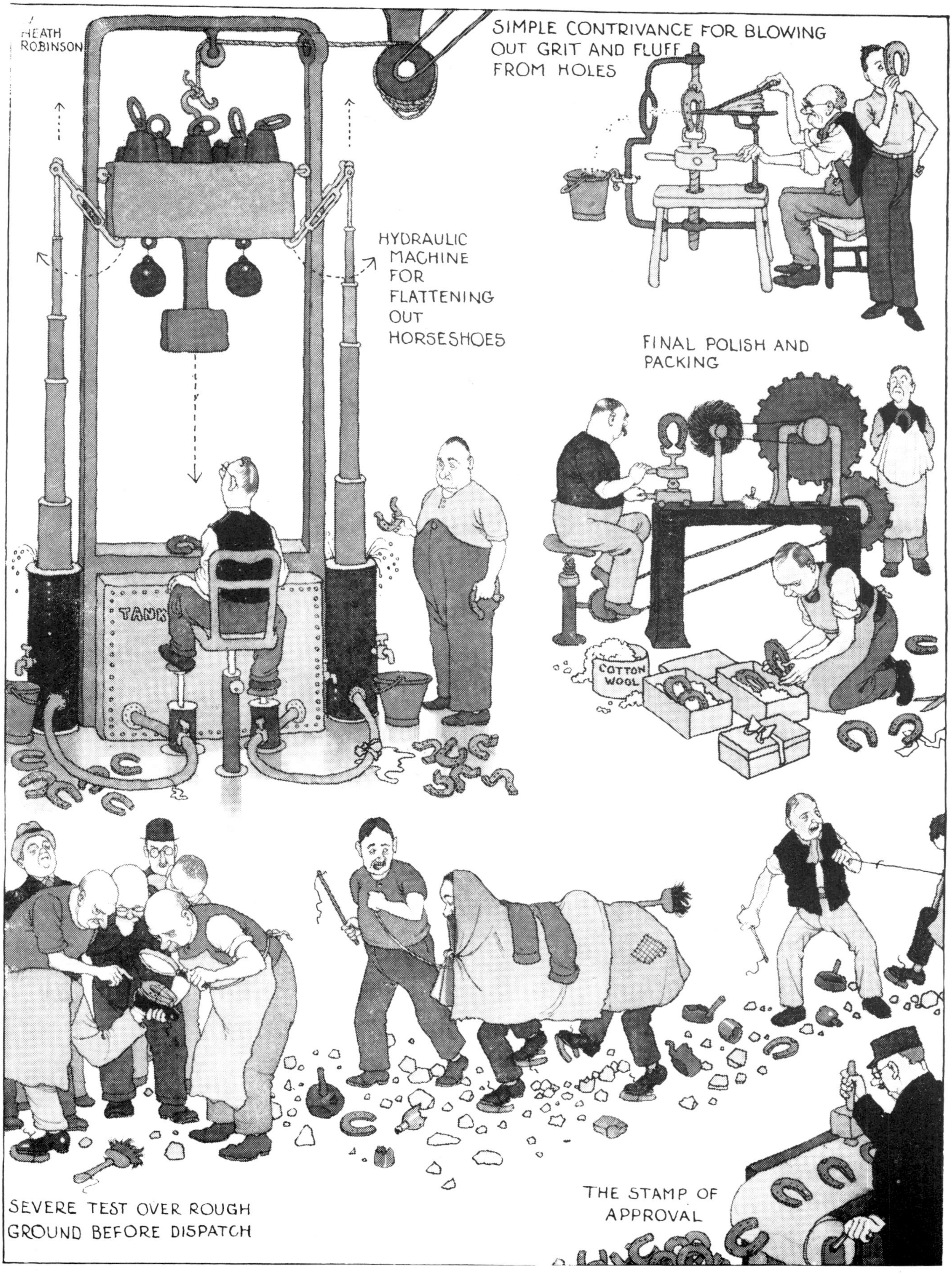

Finishing touches

Prompt Delivery

Courtesy

Committee of trained experts deciding on the best method to pursue with each drawing

The new patent air brush in use in the studio preparing a drawing for reproduction

Focussing before taking the negative

The new developing frame for rapid work with negatives

Washing and drying negatives after developing and fixing—for line, halftone, or colour reproduction

Coating the plate with a carefully mixed solution of fish glue, white of egg, etc., etc.

Conveying the impression from the negative to the sensitised plate

The etching bath. A new method of etching plates

Taking a proof

Mounting Plates on Wood for black-and-white and colour printing

SOME NEW MACHINERY FOR
PUTTING THE
FINAL TOUCHES
TO TOILET SOAP
W. HEATH
ROBINSON
A GOOD NEW YEAR'S RESOLUTION
USE WRIGHT'S COAL TAR SOAP

PLUG IN AT GREENWICH
SMITH'S SECTRIC CLOCKS
ENABLE YOU TO START ALL THE DAYS OF THE NEW YEAR ON TIME
GREENWICH
DONG
DONG
BRR R
BURR R
BRR
BRRR
BRR R R
DONG
DONG
HEATH ROBINSON

BEGIN THE NEW YEAR WELL BY JOINING
THE LONG CHAIN OF USERS OF
NUGGET
BOOT POLISH
NUGGET
"NUGGET"
REGISTERED TRADE MARK
BOOT POLISH
WATERPROOF FREE FROM ACID
THE FINEST
LEATHER PRESERVATIVE
HEATH ROBINSON

BURBERRYS New Year's Slogan
QUALITY—INDIVIDUAL AND PERSONAL ATTENTION
DETAILS
TRYING ON DEPT
HEATH ROBINSON
LEG LOWER
CHEST
LEGS LEFT RIGHT
SHOULDER LEVEL
CARRIAGE

HOW THEY COPE WITH THE
NEW YEAR'S DEMAND FOR
SHREDDED WHEAT
WASHING
THE COOKER
THE OVENS
THROUGH THE DRYING TUNNELS TO THE PACKERS
UNTOUCHED
BY HAND
THROUGHOUT
HEATH ROBINSON

LUVISCA
W HEATH ROBINSON
A New Year's Resolution —
TO MAKE QUITE CERTAIN
THAT YOUR SHIRTS and PYJAMAS
BEAR THE REGISTERED "LUVISCA" TAB
Luvisca
REGD
COURTAULDS

A GOOD RESOLUTION
W HEATH ROBINSON
GLUE
DO NOT ATTEMPT TO BUILD YOUR OWN HOUSE BUT WRITE AT ONCE TO
CO-OPERATIVE PERMANENT BUILDING SOCIETY New Oxford House London W.C.1

BY APPOINTMENT

SUPPLIERS OF DOMECQ SHERRY
LUIS GORDON & SONS LTD.

DOMECQ'S SHERRY

IMPRESSIONS OF A WELL-KNOWN SHERRY WORKS by W. HEATH ROBINSON

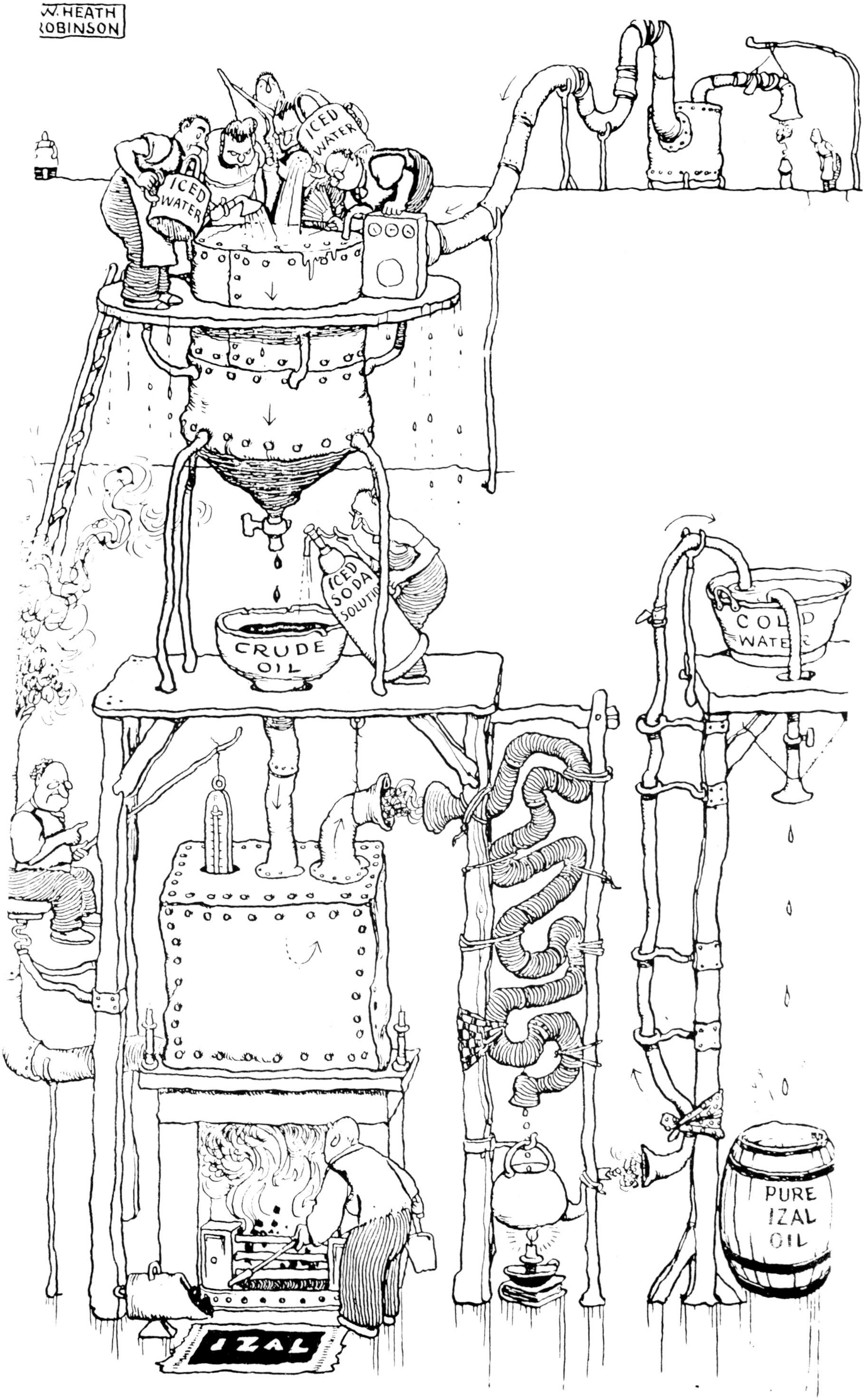
W. HEATH ROBINSON
ICED WATER
ICED WATER
ICED SODA SOLUTION
CRUDE OIL
COLD WATER
PURE IZAL OIL
IZAL

Efficient plant for the successful mixing of treated asbestos fibre with cement

Powerful machinery for conducting the mixture to the cylindrical sieves for draining off the water, whence . . .

. . . a thin film is conveyed to the cylinder upon which the sheet is built,
and this finally to the cutting machine

A patent double-action grinder for mashing the asbestos fibre

Testing Safety Matches

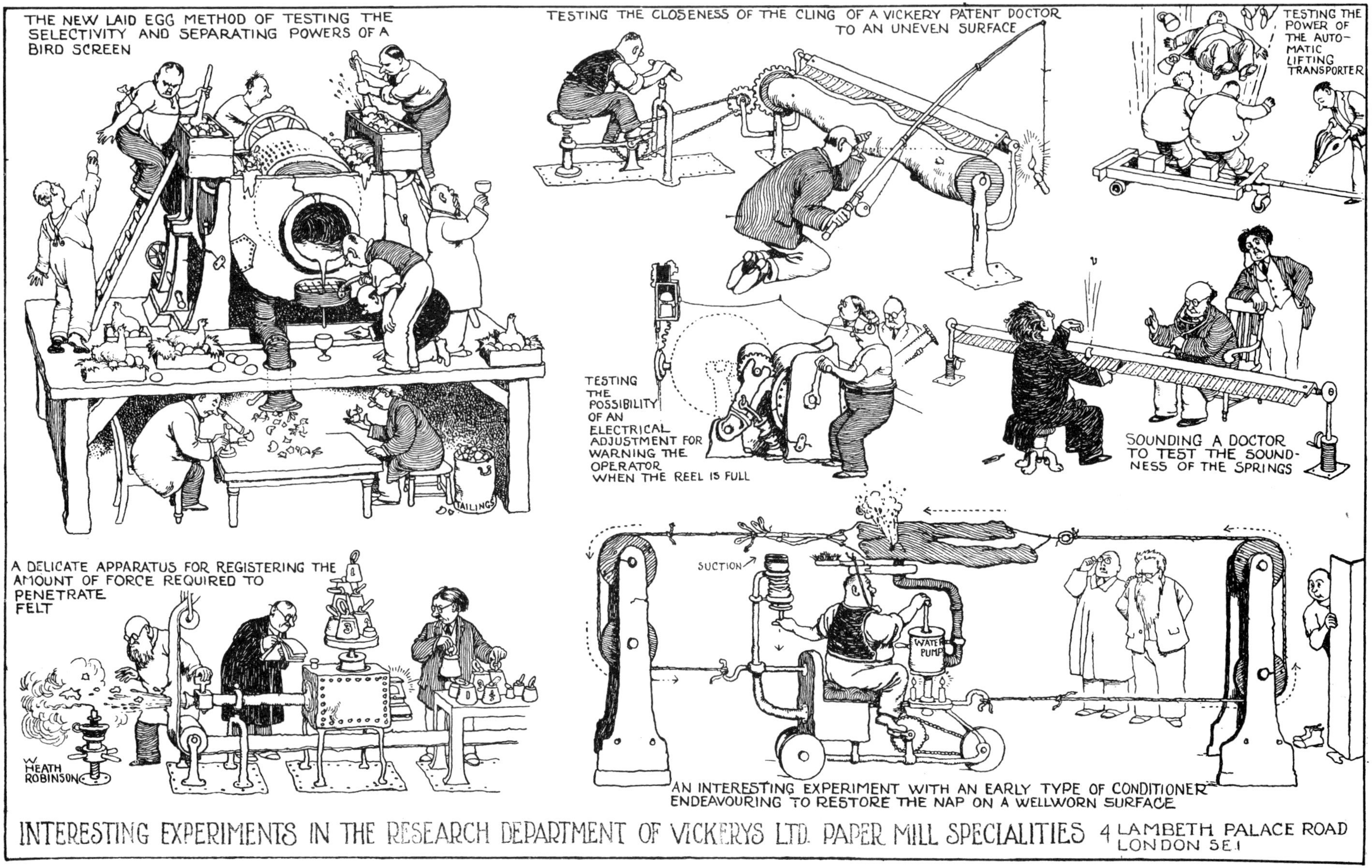
THE NEW LAID EGG METHOD OF TESTING THE SELECTIVITY AND SEPARATING POWERS OF A BIRD SCREEN
TAILINGS
TESTING THE CLOSENESS OF THE CLING OF A VICKERY PATENT DOCTOR TO AN UNEVEN SURFACE
TESTING THE POWER OF THE AUTO-MATIC LIFTING TRANSPORTER
TESTING THE POSSIBILITY OF AN ELECTRICAL ADJUSTMENT FOR WARNING THE OPERATOR WHEN THE REEL IS FULL
SOUNDING A DOCTOR TO TEST THE SOUND-NESS OF THE SPRINGS
A DELICATE APPARATUS FOR REGISTERING THE AMOUNT OF FORCE REQUIRED TO PENETRATE FELT
W. HEATH ROBINSON
SUCTION
WATER PUMP
AN INTERESTING EXPERIMENT WITH AN EARLY TYPE OF CONDITIONER ENDEAVOURING TO RESTORE THE NAP ON A WELLWORN SURFACE
INTERESTING EXPERIMENTS IN THE RESEARCH DEPARTMENT OF VICKERYS LTD. PAPER MILL SPECIALITIES 4 LAMBETH PALACE ROAD LONDON S.E.1

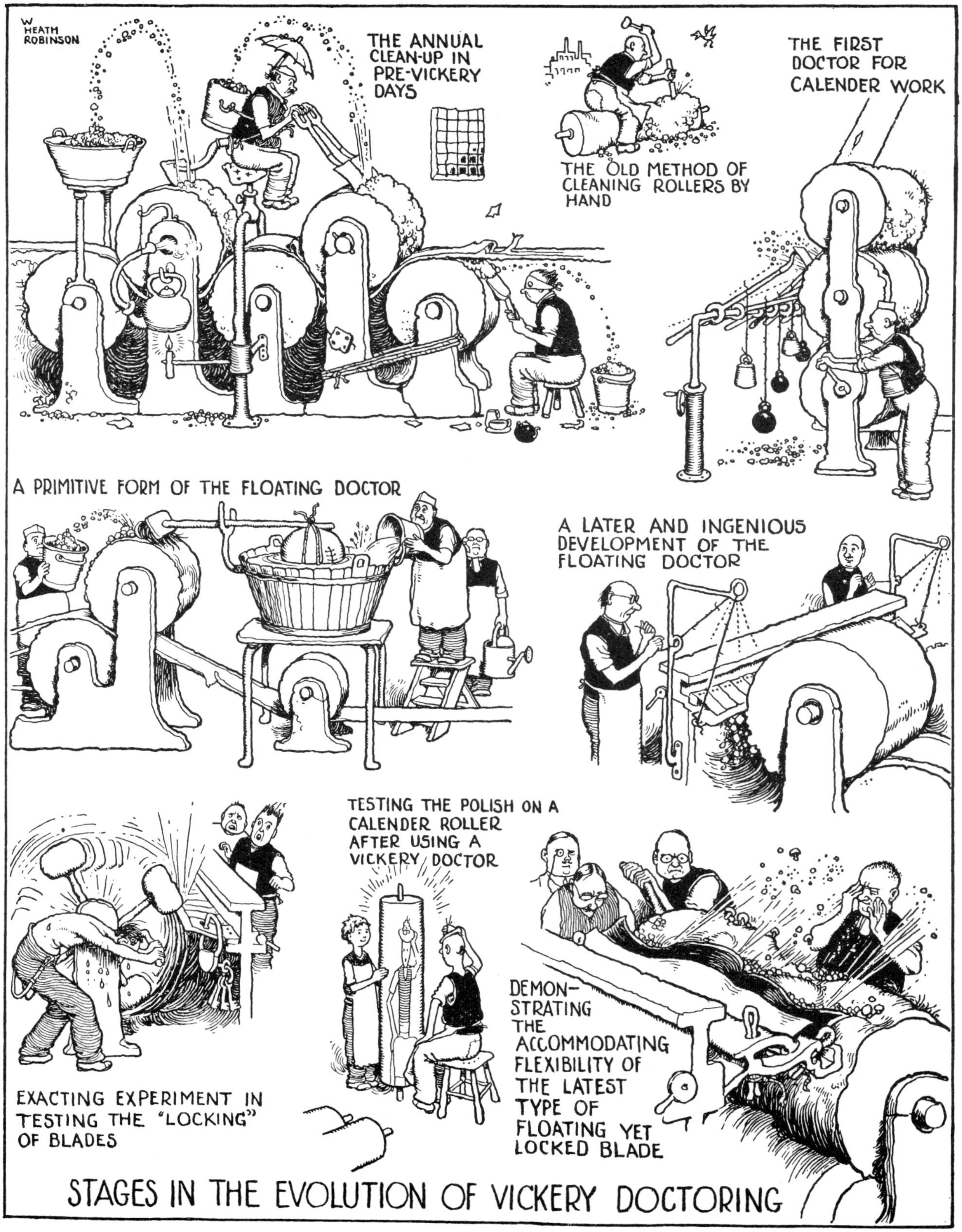
W HEATH ROBINSON
THE ANNUAL CLEAN-UP IN PRE-VICKERY DAYS
THE OLD METHOD OF CLEANING ROLLERS BY HAND
THE FIRST DOCTOR FOR CALENDER WORK
A PRIMITIVE FORM OF THE FLOATING DOCTOR
A LATER AND INGENIOUS DEVELOPMENT OF THE FLOATING DOCTOR
EXACTING EXPERIMENT IN TESTING THE "LOCKING" OF BLADES
TESTING THE POLISH ON A CALENDER ROLLER AFTER USING A VICKERY DOCTOR
DEMON-STRATING THE ACCOMMODATING FLEXIBILITY OF THE LATEST TYPE OF FLOATING YET LOCKED BLADE
STAGES IN THE EVOLUTION OF VICKERY DOCTORING

THE NEW MODEL TYPE W·H·Y·4 ROLLER

Making Down Quilts

Coke Grading

BUZZ
DUCKWORTH
PRIVATE
ENQUIRIES
WAITING
ROOM

READER
SECRETARY
EXIT
To The Consolation Dept.
W HEATH ROBINSON.